D1826139

McFadyen, Warwick
The Ocean
ISBN 978-0-646-84058-1

Published by McFadyen Media
PO Box 19 Gisborne Victoria 3437
©Warwick McFadyen 2022

Design and production: PB Publishing

The prose pieces first appeared in The
Age, The Sunday Age, The Guardian and
Footyology.com.au
Copyright resides with the author. The
moral rights of the author have been
asserted.

Photographs: Warwick McFadyen
Painting: Hamish McFadyen

A catalogue record for this
book is available from the
National Library of Australia

To Pip and Grace

The Ocean

A meditation,
in prose and poetry,
on grief

WARWICK McFADYEN

INTRODUCTION

April 10, 2022

There's the tiniest speck on the universe's calendar. It's smaller than a grain of sand in all the deserts of the world. It's invisible to the world.

It's the time from then to now: two and a half years.

Just a drop in the ocean.

But thirty months and one day, even one hour, one second, one breath ago, Hamish, my son, was still here. At some point from October 2019 onwards, the thought entered my mind via others or surfaced internally that the grieving would get better. People were trying to be kind, or perhaps I was trying to be kind to myself. By better, one meant easier.

It would get easier, the sharpness of the pain, the sudden loss of air when breathing would subside.

The grief could also be seen as a medical analogy: that like a wound, a scar would form, and in that mending of the skin would come the healing. Life grows over the scar, layer over layer.

Only time will tell. Grieving does a good trade in clichés, and why not, clichés are born in a truth. But here's another truth: memory is no substitute for the real thing. And here's another truth: the past cannot be changed.

In these years the grief has changed shape; it now has a different form. The rawness has retreated, and now a shadow has settled into the days. Sometimes, it flattens out, other times it bears a sharp edge. It's the contour of what might have been; it's the dark recesses of what has been.

This book is unfinished, necessarily so. It is not abandoned, nor is it a work in progress. The latter would imply that it is part of a movement, onwards and upwards, to improvement, that there is a final destination. But this is not a journey, though it describes an inner landscape. There can never be a terminus, for this is the landscape of grief, and love. It is carried within, and is alive as each breath signals life. This is the terrain of loss.

This is a gathering of words, over three years, of a father to a son.

Hamish McFadyen
1998-2019

CONTENTS

FLOOD

December 2019
(Two months)

When my dear son's heart stopped

Every day I stare into the abyss, and say good morning. Before sleep, I go to it again and say good night, adding, See you in the morning. The abyss sits on a shelf.

Sometimes, I reach up to it, and slightly touch its edge. Just to know that it is real, that it exists and that this is not a dream without sense. I tell the abyss that I love it. I love it so much my heart breaks. For before it became the abyss it had another name.

Hamish. My son.

Hamish died in October. He was 21. His heart failed, as all hearts do. But in one just starting out in life, the anguish of early death is telescoped into a dense black star of what might have been, should have been.

It sits dead in our hearts.

After the first monstrous waves of black grief smash you into the sand, again and again, the tide has receded. First you are left numb, time is divided into real and not real. My wife and daughter, we three, riding a sea of tears and memory. These are but the early days of grief, I know, a life of loss is stretching forever.

After the furious storms and gales of lament that howled against heart and mind, a surface calm is developing and a stone, weightier than the earth is sinking within the ocean of the soul: that is death and love.

Hamish should have been on the funeral dais in 40 years, speaking of his dear old man, dead at 101, But that would have given life a fairness, and life is not fair. I spoke at his funeral. This is what I said:

Words aren't enough.

I'm not much of a talker, but I'm a good listener, and now I keep listening for his voice, just two words, Hey Dad. And they'll never come to me again. But I can talk to him, and of him here, among friends and family. He is with us, within us, and we are with him.

When Hamish was living in St Kilda, he would phone me and say Hey Dad, I've just written a couple of poems, can I read them to you? Or he would text: Hey dad, got a poem I just wrote down at the park that'll be waiting for you (whenever I was next coming down). Excellent, I'd say, You're on fire. He'd reply, Hopefully it's a long streak haha. They were good, too.

It was too brief a blooming. At primary school he was picked to take part in the Gateways program for gifted children in writing in Melbourne. In high school he earned distinctions in the University of NSW school competitions in English/ Writing.

We'd talk about his poems in the past year, and I'd say mate send me copies. Yeah, yeah, he'd say, today or tomorrow, might just do some work on them. There was always tomorrow. You're 21. Of course, there's always tomorrow.

We like to kid ourselves there'll always be tomorrow.

Hamish and I went overseas a few years back.

One night in Paris he read me some other poems he had written and I told him, Sorry to have to tell you this mate, but you're a poet and you're going to be poor for the rest of your life. We laughed. He hated being broke.

John Cooper Clarke was a favourite, especially the haiku:

> *To freeze the moment*
> *In seventeen syllables*
> *Is very diffic.*

And alongside that he read someone like Seamus Heaney. Everything flows. Even a solid man.

One late afternoon we sat on the banks of the Seine just down from Notre Dame. It was spring, beautiful light and a warmth on the skin. We were having a beer just like all the other Parisians seemed to be doing. We were smiling, soaking up the last rays of the day. It didn't get any better than this, we toasted life.

If we were talking about life, the state of the world, or music or films, Hamish would throw in insights into whatever the topic was and open up the discussion wider than I had thought it could go. So many times I would say, You're right. I hadn't thought of that, and he would get a half grin on his face.

He had that same half grin when I showed him a note his sister had written to him that I had found recently. They were both quite young, and after a morning or afternoon of brotherly-sisterly torment, she felt she needed to tell Hamish this: Hamish, sometimes I wish I didn't have a brother, but I was wrong, you're the best little brother a sister could wish for.

He kept it in a frame on his desk.

Fate can so cruelly mock, for Hamish had a good heart. He was, at heart, gentle and loving. He had the most joyous laugh. When he was younger he played soccer with a grace of movement and a speed that was wonderful to watch, and then he took that movement and speed to the skatepark. He was fearless on a skateboard. There were take-offs from ramps that had perpendicular drops. No problem.

I'd stand at the edge, an old surfer, and I'd pull back. Not him.

Around the same time, he was with two other friends in a power trio, they played on the back of a truck at Gisborne market one Sunday morning, belting out the Beatles and Green Day. He was the drummer. Again that movement, that rhythm. He had the longest fingers. I used to joke that guitarists would kill to have his hands. Again, he laughed. They were for the drums.

Once in the search for the perfect skate bowl, we went to deepest, darkest Sunshine for the perfect bowl. It was inside a warehouse that looked like a set from Terminator. He loved it. I just kept an eye out for cyborgs. He also fell for, shall we say, exterior painting. Though he also got into painting on small canvas.

One day he just sat down in the sunroom and tossed off a water colour of a small, beautiful blue bird. We could have it, he said. It wasn't quite finished to him.

And now the axis of our world has tilted. How can the earth keep turning, how can the day break and the night fall, without him?

How can the birds sing, and the moon rise, the waves come to shore and the stars shine constant, without him?

Everything flows. Between nothingness and eternity, there is life.

Precious life. If you're lucky, love will nestle into your arms, like Hamish did first born, as a baby, as a toddler, as child and still in our minds, growing up. We were lucky beyond one can dare to dream. We had Hamish, and he had us. He still has us. He always will. We loved him beyond words.

When I picked him up from the funeral director's home, I strapped him into the front seat. To be safe. Always wear your seatbelt, mate, I said. Always the father. Forever the father.

In the weeks after, I wrote this:

The Horizon

From the river
To the sea
The sky awaits
Each drop of rain
To return
Into the silence.
I dip my hand in
and out of the water.
The tide is
Leaving me.
Droplets cling to my skin.
I look to the sky
And write
On its surface
With my hand:
His name is
Hamish.

These days, I tell myself that the abyss sometimes answers my greeting, I know Dad. Love you too.

February 2020
(Four months)

Time passes, taking love deeper

I don't keep a diary. I tried in high school, but found that, not unexpectedly, my life was somewhat less than exciting and certainly not worth recording.

When I was a global traveller in my twenties I never tagged the photographs with place and date. I won't forget where that is, or who they are, I thought at the time. Ah the conceit of youth that memories won't fade. Places and people, quite a few are strangers to me now.

But this. Now the days are a diary of a life lost. Some days, the writing is faint, barely visible, others deep, engraved. It was the week before Christmas, The Age published a piece I had written about the loss of my son Hamish. Now it's . . . .

Four months.
Each day is a step further away.

From him, my son.
Four months and a couple of weeks
in the calculus of grief.
The precision of loss, the dissection of time:
21 years gone in the closing blink of an eye.
In a few days he would have been 22.

But this is not a poem. This is the shortened carriages of thought from brain and heart that arrive and depart. It's a constant movement of emotional freight. There is no timetable. No arriving on the hour, departing on the half hour: the trigger and the release. Grief has no clockwork. It comes and goes as it pleases. It is the visitor of ill-content.

This is the time after the time. This is the levelling out of grief.

How are you? Once, before October 2019, the answer was simple. Yeah, fine, all things being equal.

Four months on, and the question assumes a challenging aspect. It drags death from the shadows to front and foremost. It sits like a drop of mercury in your open palm. How to grasp it and give it form. For in its definition resides your answer.

It was easier to answer in the hollowed hours at the time. You were desolate. You were in a landscape where life and time stood still. It was ground zero of the soul. You didn't have to answer, most could see it in your eyes, in the crack of your voice as you thought, how can I answer that. Most people really didn't expect an answer, indeed, many said, No words.

How are you now? I am how I was, but I am not how I was. Four months is a short timescale on which to measure emotional equilibrium. Indeed, how can you measure this ocean? You can never be how you had once been. You can go to the classics: Shakespeare, "Love is not love which does alter when it alteration finds,/Or bends with the remover to remove./O no! it is an ever-fixed mark/That looks on tempests and is never shaken."

Or Rainer Maria Rilke. The poet, who measured life as a constant becoming of self-realisation wedded to the universe, wrote that death did not exceed our strength.

In a letter to Sidonie Nadherna von Borutin, whose brother had died, Rilke wrote: "Your letter really touches my heart. On the one hand, I want to encourage you in your pain so that you will completely experience it in all its fullness, because as the experience of a new intensity it is a great experience and leads everything back again to life, like everything that reaches a certain degree of greatest strength.

"But on the other hand I am very concerned when I imagine how strangled and cut off you currently live, afraid of touching anything that is filled with memories (and what is not filled with memories?)

"You will freeze in place if you remain this way. You must not."

Life moves on. Four months. Ground zero still exists, will forever more.

Now, How are you? is marked by the ticking of the clock on the wall, the schedule of daily life, the bills that must be paid, the shopping that must be done, the dog that must be walked, the lawn that must be mowed, the day that must be greeted, the work that gives you form, the absence that lives within you, the love that stays the silence.

The question often can be triggered by the rising of ghosts, at the soccer fields where he used to play, the skate park where he used to ride (In a wanton act of vandalism I graffitied "H sk8ted here" in permanent marker). Or it can arise from ordinary conversation. It's the unknowing How are you?

When a conversation with a stranger serving you in a shop somehow turns to families and you're asked do you have kids, yes you reply, a daughter and a son. Where do you go if you say a daughter. And once I had a son. He died.

There's no point in turning a stranger's innocent smiling question into awkward silence. You take your leave, and let the lie remain the easier answer.

Some days, most days, in the first tidal movements of grief, I would say aloud to myself, to the air: Hamish is dead. This was mostly when I would take the dog for a morning walk. I would stop and utter the phrase. No one was listening, but me. I was the audience. I was the one who needed to say the words and hear them, to take them in. To take deep breaths.

Where are you if you are not here, I would ask. I knew the answer. He was nowhere. And if he was wasn't here then where was I? I was among the living. For life goes on. I don't say it so often now. I know. I know.

In January, we spent a few weeks in Tasmania at the coastal town where we used to go for family holidays.

I used to joke that the cold water builds character, as son and daughter shivered walking into the ocean. One day I'll take you both to a beach where the water is warm. One day.

One day this January I walked on the same beach, deserted as it was in the dusk, and wrote the letter H in the sand. My wife wrote a message too nearby. I knew the tide would wash them away. But in the action was the memory. And in these days does it flow deeper and stronger.

September 2020
(Twelve months)

The flame of a candle

The one and only tall glass in the house had dropped to the floor, broken into pieces.

And so it was a few weeks ago I opened the door to the homewares store in our town. It would have tall unbroken glasses. The store was part temple, part catalogue of the moderne. The sound of chimes and keyboards, gentle and soothing, washed over me; sweet-smelling vapours rose up, swirled in the air.

This was a place where the new age had become normal. If the crockery and cutlery could speak it would be in mantras of serenity. We will serve you well they might intone. Life was calm in here, life was ordered, a place for everything and everything in its place.

Where might the long, tall glasses be I asked the chimes, for there seemed to be no one else in the store. Do these appeal? they asked, as I walked past long-stemmed wine glasses.

The wafting scents of new ageism must have been transporting me to fields of lavender, but I snapped out of it at the sight of the tall glasses.

Excellent, now to be gone.

But the aura held me. I wondered lonely as a cloud, for still no one had appeared, would anyone frame an entire home in these colours and airs? Function had become lifestyle. Still, I was here so what did that say about me? It said the supermarket didn't have any and this place did.

And it was in this place of designer ware, a crack in the glass appeared. This glass wasn't on display. It wasn't on the shelves. I carry it around within. The glass and the fracturing. One is the love, the other is the loss.

This glass carries an ocean. It rises and falls. Sometimes, the crack is the smallest rend in the surface, other times it is a shattering on the ground.

I always pick up the pieces, or try to; and maybe there are shards still where they have fallen. I could have missed picking up all the broken bits. It's possible. Anything is possible now, one year on.

The glass has a name. Hamish.

As I waited for someone to appear from the backroom, where I could hear boxes being moved about, I was accompanied around the shelves by the meandering melodies, that is aimlessly, and that is where the aroma and the music coalesced into an evocation of another time I had been here.

Memory triggered.

But unlike those memories triggered by a song from your youth that immediately takes you back to the time, or a smell or a sight that carries you to a place, this trigger became a realisation, became the crack appearing. I was looking for candles. It was October last year. I didn't know what I was looking for in the candles but this: dignity, and a flame that would mean more than its light and heat.

However that can be done. Perhaps that's where the flame watchers come in — to see and feel in its essence something else, to give it a meaning beyond its essence.

The candles would only be used once. They would sit atop the coffin wherein lay the body of my son. They would flicker and fade, and then be gone. I don't know where they are now. Not with us, but in memory.

I thought I had started to know the grief-stricken landscape, had travelled enough times by the places where the triggers would most likely go off to be prepared for the shot to be felt.

But this is a landscape where the sun and shadows keep moving, and the click of heartache in your breast is but a breath away.

"H skated here. He was good." The words I wrote on the skate park ramp after the funeral have faded now into the concrete. No one, especially young kids, would know its significance. But I do. I took my misnamed permanent marker back there recently and wrote it again. I go past the skate park almost each morning with the dog.

Sometimes it's a trigger to memories, other times not. Some mornings he is whistling down the ramp, other times there is only silence.

The day before this past Father's Day I was sitting at my desk. My iPod (I'm that vintage) was on song shuffle. There are more than 7000 tracks on the iPod.

An acoustic guitar being strummed came out of the speakers. And then a young boy, probably 11 or 12, said, "Is this in a different tuning?" A voice I recognised as mine replied, "Yeah, sorry about that."

The boy, "Arrrggghhhhh!" Then silence.

The track clicked off.

It was Hamish.

Memory triggered. I can picture the exchange from a decade ago. It was in the sunroom, mid-afternoon. There was lightness in the room. I had forgotten I had left the record button on while I was playing into the mini-recorder. Sometime after I must have transferred the afternoon's doodlings to the iPod. Now, it's a sentence to treasure.

I still have his voice.

A song can transport you to another country within the hemisphere of your life.

You can be pulled back there, remember, I once lived here, for a time, perhaps allow yourself a smile or laugh, but you know, of course, that now you don't.

And soon the biggest trigger is but a matter of days away. Soon will come the explosion and the creation of a black hole.

Among the chimes and scented air I was transported back to four candles lit for a life. And a crack appeared in the glass.

This was not the ringing glass that shatters as it rings. It ran through the sunlight of the day and vanished until the next trigger memory.

I took my bought glass home, filled it with water and drank to the flame of a candle that cannot be **extinguished.**

October 10, 2021
(Two years)

Time stood still

There are shadows within the shadows. There is breath within the breath. There are words within the words.

While I might have had intimations of these things, from a philosophical aspect, the past two years have taught me this in the way of moonlight seeping into my bones.

Before October 2019, time's straight arrow was just that. It had no other dimension to it. Now the arrow is both real and illusion.

Just a few months before the Earth shifted on its axis when a virus departed China to travel the world and wreak more than 4.5 million deaths upon it, an axis of love broke. A world within the world broke its moorings, never to return.

And, unbeknown to me, a new language was forming to try to define the meaning of it all. This was time giving shape to loss. It began two years ago, when time stopped.

Two hourglasses now sit within me. In one the grains of sand continue to flow, seconds, to hours, to days. In the other, the sand is frozen, its grains suspended.

This dichotomy now courses through my blood, leaves my heart and, contrary to physiology, returns. It is the cycle of life and death, of memory and grief, of tide, shoreline and horizon. The moment this began was in my son's last breath. Hamish was 21.

I've written at intervals in these past two years of the grief and the memory. The words were the emanation from a deep well. I can no more stop the flow then stop the hours. It has felt in its non-rational way a means of keeping my son alive that if there were words rather than ash the pain would be less. Something to hold on to, the heart demanded it, never mind the head.

In those first weeks, the words were drawn from a wound raw and a pulse relentless in lament. People speak of time as the great healer — as a comfort and solace, but it is also frightening for its healing resides in the only tool it has, putting distance between the living and the dead. It can be no other way, of course. Life goes on.

And yet. And yet. In the moving forward, there has been a

shift in the gears of grief. Not so much akin to a tremor of the mindscape but a sway in the looking of the clouds passing in the sky. There is an elemental change in the definition of grief. At once, I hate it, but know it is undeniable. My son's life is receding.

The here and now of him is like a small boat sailing from me on an ocean too wide and deep to hold it back. Sometimes, in the ever-widening parting of the years I think I can hear him say, let go dad, I'm gone. And this is the hardest part. For he is right, and memory is no substitute really for the here and now. Yet it being all there is, standing before the great maw of forever, one holds it dear. One holds it close, and thanks time for having had the love at all. How lucky is that among the vastness of the universe?

Rilke wrote in Requiem for a Friend: "We need, in love, to practise only this:/letting each other go/For holding on comes easily;/we do not need to learn it."

The words are easier to write than act upon. Rilke never had a son.

In the latter months words have become more distillation. The prose has become poems. The road travelled to a finished poem is a strange journey, for words are more discarded than used. A poem is naked. The links in the chain of words seem more intense and more closely entwined in the distilling of feeling to keep the circle from breaking. It's ironic I should describe the virtues of the poem in a prose piece, but there you are.

This is one of the poems:

The Wake

The surface breaks and in the parting
lines of ripples slip away.
They crest then fade into the fold
that swirls and sleeps under the spray.

This is the lapping of each moment
from rock of cradle to silent grave,
this is the voice that no longer travels
but for what it left and what it gave.

This is the widening wake, carrying
the echo and call of a life now past
to my shore-bound days. The water
runs through my hands. I hold it fast.

Two years ago, time stopped. And yet as Shakespeare wrote "Like as the waves make towards the pebbled shore/So do our minutes hasten to their end". True enough. Death is a certainty. And yet, time continues, and we go with its currents. I like to think that swimming in this ocean, waiting for the next wave, he is next to me, shouting, Go for it, Dad.

And then this …
(May 4, 2022)

For the past 30 months I have swum in an ocean, my head bobbing above the water line, have felt the splash and thud of waves, the sting of salt, the dragging further out from land, the nursing back to shore, the ebb and flow of heartache. The ocean is a part of me.

So now, the ocean has a name: prolonged grief disorder. Its depths, its shoals, its islands within it, its breadth, its currents, its horizons. Prolonged grief disorder.

My state of heart has been diagnosed, courtesy of the American Psychiatric Association. Not specifically, of course. But in general terms, it's in a state of disorder. Except, it's not. Its state is the natural flow of love, the river of life, where all life flows, to the ocean.

All of us carry it within their own particular ocean when they are intimately touched by a death, especially the death of a child.

In October 2019 my son Hamish died. He was 21. His loss is my ocean. His life, like a river, ran through mine. I grieve him now, as I did from the first second of his passing; the shape of the grief changing as time goes on. I will grieve him always for where once there was his life in mine, now there is his death. It's not a prolongation, as if there is a clock calling time on appropriate exercising of mourning.

How do you measure such things, by callipers, ultrasounds, x-rays, electrocardiograms, blood samples?

According to the association's Diagnostic and Statistical Manual of Mental Disorders (DSM-5), which was released recently, people who are still grieving a year after the loss, and are unable to walk back into their daily life, as it was before the death, have prolonged grief disorder.

A report in The New York Times says that with the diagnosis now in the DSM-5 doctors who are treating people with the disorder can invoice insurance companies. It will also lead, of course, to a race by pharmaceutical companies to provide medication to treat it.

Naltrexone, which is prescribed among other uses, to block the effects of heroin, is being tested clinically as grief therapy. Naltrexone's side effects might include anxiety and sleep problems.

The Times report quotes Joanne Cacciatore, an associate professor at Arizona State University, who has written on grief. She is wary of the move. "I completely, utterly disagree that grief is a mental illness. When someone who is a quote-unquote 'expert' tells us we are disordered and we are feeling very vulnerable and feeling overwhelmed, we no longer trust ourselves and our emotions. To me, that is an incredibly dangerous move, and short-sighted."

Dangerous, and deaf to the murmurings of the soul, that is the essence of being human. To give it a label, a disorder, is to give it the stain of abnormality. Something that needs to be cleansed. It says, for you to live, to move on, you must disinfect yourself.

Paul Appelbaum, chairman of the committee that oversaw the inclusion of the diagnosis in DSM-5, put it like this: the people recognised as having such a disorder "were the widows who wore black for the rest of their lives, who withdrew from social contacts and lived the rest of their lives in memory of the husband or wife who they had lost. They were the parents who never got over it, and that was how we talked about them. Colloquially, we would say they never got over the loss of that child."

Indeed, Mr Appelbaum. Indeed.

Grief, surely, is part of the order of life and death. To consider it as akin to a pathology is wrong in every way you look at it. Take grief out of the landscape that is left after you have lost someone you love, and what is left? The barren earth, the sky without hope. To lament is to love even when the object of that love has gone. This is grieving. It is not a disorder of the mind.

To go down that path would be akin to creating a pathology of grief.

Many cultures over centuries have brought grief into their way of life, into their rituals. It is a grain of their human harvest, a thread of their tapestry. In Mexico, there is a celebration called the Day of the Dead, a three-day festival where the departed are welcomed back. It is held every year.

This is how the Royal College of Pathologists of Australasia defines pathology: "Pathology is the medical specialty concerned with the study of the nature and causes of diseases."

Grief is not a disease. Grief is the ocean. It is Hamish, his life and death writ in water.

It is love remembered. Apologies to e.e. cummings, I carry his heart with me (I carry it in my heart) I am never without it.

Memory visible
(September 24, 2022)

I am walking in the graveyard, among the cedars, oaks and pines, among the dead. I'd like to say it's quiet, which of course it is — that's its nature — but it is also bordered on two sides by roads. Life motors by in a wake of sound.

But here life is brought to a halt, and in the halting silence, family roots go deep. Among the cedars, oaks and pines are the markers to eternity, the plaques, headstones and crosses, and behind each one a funeral, and before that, a life.

The cemetery is on a little hill — what would have been the edge of town when hill became graveyard in 1858. It was first divided according to faith — as in life, so too death — and now it has a non-denominational section.

A memorial remembers the children and adults in unmarked graves: 350 kids and 341 adults, according to the burial register. They are not lost or forgotten, the memorial whispers.

As I walk, there's a whispering, too, in my heart: where, what type, but mainly there is how to place memory in stone?

Soon among the oaks, a plaque on stone will be laid alongside the other plaques. It will bear my son's name. He died three years ago. In the giant yaw of that time, the eternity of one day opened up like a flower.

Walking in this graveyard, improbably, T.S. Eliot walked besides me: "Between the idea/And the reality/Between the motion/And the act/Falls the Shadow (For Thine is the Kingdom)/Between the conception/And the creation/ Between the emotion/And the response/Falls the Shadow (Life is very long)."

Yet life was not long for our son. He was 21. We have kept his ashes close, storing how to mark his passing in the same place as his urn – on a shelf, waiting for night's descent to become merely shadow, to become the remains of that day. But now we are ready.

We have met a cemetery trust representative to decide on a marker on a hill in a town he was born into and where he died. His place is on the edge of a garden bed. It's sheltered, and a park bench is opposite the stone where the plaque will be mounted. It's close enough for our words to float onto his name without being blown away. Of course, no gale, no gust could do that. Distance now means nothing, being without measure. We hold each other close, tears well up and fall, and we nod, yes this is the place.

He'd like it here. It's a consolation of grief for parents.

Perpetuity has a price tag, as it must, for it exists in the present day. A graveyard must be well cared for, lawns mown, garden beds maintained. And there are different tiers of mourning. The bigger the marker the greater the cost. The cosmos would wink at that. Perhaps it's whispering too: have faith, I have more perpetuity than you'll ever need.

Even the grandest monuments will one day grow moss, their words chiselled down by wind and rain. All you can really ask is for a little more time. But graveyards are the great leveller. Time rubs against the skin of everyone.

This, then, is the utter last stop, where ash becomes earth, the final accounting of a life, the letting go. His ashes will go beneath the plaque — the heart, the smile, the laughter, the boy entire of love — to earth.

And within us there is the invisible, unbreakable thread without measure, the echo of love.

That night

Someone asks me my name, an ambulance officer I think.

"War……" I'm drowning. I can't say my own name. My voice is breaking. His name is Hamish, I say.

DISTILLATION

Flow

Empty this into my heart —
The sky, the infinite surface,
let me feel when I look within
that I am looking out as well.

Empty this into my heart —
The wash and whorl of the sea
let me feel the tide's pull and push
of moonlight and shadow.

Empty this into my heart —
The light of distant stars
that I might hold close the wisp
of time that I can say is only mine.

Empty this into my heart —
The whisper of wind on worn stone
that I can listen, and return it
in a voice, never emptying.

THE WAIT
(Father to son)

Here now
– coming.

Exchange
typed
of flesh
and blood.

Here now
– coming.
Call and
response
now ghost
words.

Here now
– coming.

The empty
screen,
the silence
of ash.

Here now
– coming.
Here now
– coming.

Every day he walks
inhaling
the infinity
of the sky.
It's an exercise
of the mind:
If he keeps
walking,
maybe he'll run
into him.
Maybe he'll come
full circle,
before zero
became eternity.

Here now
– coming.

No more.
In the here
and now.

The Door

Once I could open this door
though I can see it still.

I could greet the eyes,
touch the skin.

Once I could open this door
and words would meet.

At beginning and end
the door knows only

that it opens, shuts,
silently stands.

Time was, was once time
that I could open this door

believing I had all the time
in my hands, in the world.

No one has all the time,
the hinge on the door
swings open, swings shut
without us, within us.

The Second Christmas

A crow caws
in a captured sky,
it rises and dives
in a flickering eye.

Its wings bring
the flutter of
a darkness deep —
but I am love

it says, though
of the hardest kind;
by the restless air my wings
to your heart bind.

I take your
breath in wisp and wave,
release it to the stars —
knowing none can save

the drawing
of more, for the flow
is a promise of memory
that will not slow.

I exist,
it says, because one does not.
I live within the space
of a caprice, a knot
that takes shape
without reasons
or order to the rhyme
of the fixed seasons.

A phoenix
I am not; I cannot give
rise to what has been lost
nor my birth forgive

the power
of caws and effect;
a language run wordless —
not of meanings' neglect

 — but of what
I am. For in your soul
I now reside forever, the
missing part of the whole.

Intimations

Through shade of tree
and light of sun
the path leads,

A rustle of meditation
whispers, *There will always*
                    be time.

There
     will
         not
            be
               time
                    sighs
                         a
                            cloud.

Under heavens that spark,
in the days that flicker
            in the scrape

of worlds against worlds
go I: incantation and
                inhalation.

Intimations wash over my eyes
like rolling waves breaking
                    into foam.

Till human voices wake us,
and we drown.

No, it is not that.

But this: each voice is a
constellation, a flash of comets,
                    and fixed stars

flaring and fading out
the breath rises, then dies,
            within the chambers

that we carry; our universe,
a sky bruised with hope;
  this is our love song.

And the path is a coil of the heart
that sings from the warmth
     of the sun.

We walk in the shade.

We walk in the light.

The Rockpool

Where sea meets shore
there is a hollow
in the rock that cradles
the ocean's leaving.

In its shallows,
like a memory,
the wash of the depths
is briefly held.
For storms may visit
the rough flush
of wilding waves
upon its core

And take the thing
itself but, in the
taking, redeem
anew a part of itself.

Becalmed, silent,
kissed by the waves
of the sun, it offers
reflection like a prayer.

Ocean and pool
coalesce, from
horizon's edge
to hollow in rock.

In the receding is the
return.

The Unbreaking Wave

Not as a flower holds light,
but as the wave
that never breaks
the sky holds infinity.

Not as we hold time
nestling in flesh and bone,
but as the sigh of the stars,
the sky holds infinity.

Not as a promise to us,
but as the mirror
that reflects upon itself,
the sky holds infinity.
The sky holds infinity,
not for our purpose,
but we carry this:

for each pin of light
that falls to earth
we transform
the untouchable
into the touched.

A small thread
of luminescence
we go, a flower cast
upon the wave.

Winter is Upon the Earth

The light that bore summer
within it is fading
and reforming;
less of the sun,
more of the moon.
Like a tide going out
and returning,
ice-capped:
winter is upon us.

Residing within
the turning days
that move through
blood, flesh and bone.

At times, rising as a storm
carrying bruised clouds
or settling as a frozen pond
at the bottom of the still heart.
A guest that cannot be turned away.
The chill air slaps our senses awake;
we fold warmth into our hands,
blow on them to keep it alive.
In a darkened season, in this
pale light, we look for a path.

The Leaving
(When spring comes)

Oaks once slumbering
stretch their limbs
in the spring air,
the earth underfoot
pulses with
awakening life.

Light pours in,
where once
it glistened
on the rim
of frost-touched
mornings.

As if bent from a magnet's
attraction, the light now
casts shadows out
of silence and sways
not the rhythm
of the season but the heart.

Another anniversary blooms
unwanted, uncalled.
This is the untended garden
of tireless love and memory
where the young roots taunt:
we will never die.
For we have become the sap rising,
and the colours turning,
the veins of the new leaf,
and the leaf falling.
We have entered the bloodstream
and made the heart our home.

In the widening of the years,
in the turning of the seasons
the distance grows, we age
while zero remains zero.
This is the equation of loss.
This is the long leaving.

The Wake

The surface breaks and in the parting
lines of ripples slip away.
They crest then fade into the fold
that swirls and sleeps under the spray.

This is the lapping of each moment
from rock of cradle to silent grave,
this is the voice that no longer travels
but for what it left and what it gave.

This is the widening wake, carrying
the echo and call of a life now past
to my shore-bound days. The water
runs through my hands. I hold it fast.

The Hours

I tried to hold the hours in my hand
but I couldn't make a fist of it.

And yet I wait for light of sun,
crest of moon to fall into its grasp

and coalesce as prayer that day's
shadow will not lengthen as

time demands it must. In the end,
everything becomes nothing to it.

But between those two points
the open hand tries to keep close

a distance further than star and moon.
This is loss for love immeasurable.

This is the soul's timepiece:
My heart knows this my heart.

Another Graveyard

I didn't mean to be among
the bones and ash
of the graveyard cradling
life gone and memory fixed.
The clouds pulled me, the sun
guided me, to flowers in vases,
to the worn edges of stone
and the dried tears of farewell.
Among the oaks and turned soil
settling into eternity,
headstones and plaques sigh
among themselves; each a life,
now folded into words and dates,
each an etching on the passing years,
while unmarked graves, of adult
and child, go unremarked.

Divided by path and patches of lawn
death has its order: by alphabet
and by boundaries of tribes
who believe they know
the contours of the darkness
after it falls. I sit in the sunlight
and shadows and know only this:
visitors all, we are borne on the breeze.

And are gone.

Into the grain

This tree grows
from roots seen
and unseen.
Higher, wider
it rises
branching,
wilting,
blooming,
shearing.

Life and death
run in its veins;
rain and drought
seep into the fibres
that colour the grain
that shape its spine,
one to give, one to
take, both part of
creation's cycle.

This tree bends
in the high wind,
takes the gusts
and gales of storms
with the fall
of shadows and sun
across its leaf.
It carries the weather
in its arms.

But still the bough
can break,
the trunk can topple.
It has no shield
strong enough to stop
the snap of its roots
no matter how far
they reach
into the earth.

And yet, this tree grows
from the words
that form in a deep
well and rise to enter
in the grain of your life.
Love, always love.

Incantation

The jewels you hold close
are not the ones you wear.
The light in your eyes
is not the glow of gems.
The sound of your voice
is not the cut of stone.
The touch of your hand
is not the grasp of gold.
The taste on your lips
is not the silver rim.
The jewels you hold close
have no value, but to
you. They cannot be
stolen and then resold.

Their shape is the wave
forming and reforming
from the undertow
that runs through your heart.

The jewels you hold close
are the first cry, the last
tear, the sigh of love
and the silence of loss.
They enter the blood
unbeholden to time.

The jewels hold you close;
never leaving, for they
are what you receive,
forever enfolding.

Your soul's shoreline in
quiet transformation.

Bejewelled.

The Light That Travels

It was bin night — yellow and green
I placed them on the kerb
and, walking back to the house,
I looked up into the night sky
and tried to read the stars
left to right and back again;
a stream of centuries' light
had travelled to me in the blackness,
in the ordinary rituals. On bin night.
Thank you, I said, as quiet as star dust.

I knew my words could not rise
to the stars. They fell fading to earth
or were borne away on a swirl of air.
Yet they stayed with me; a pulse,
an echo in the heart's chamber.

The stars that night were not mine,
though I held their distance close;
scientists may give them names,
while we see what we dream them to be.
On bin night — yellow and green
I looked up into the night sky
and knew that even as one star died,
its light still travelled through
the emptiness and nestled
in my eyes, on bin night, until
I too would return to dust.

So It Goes

It's hard not to ask
looking up at the sky
In all of the vastness,
Where is the I?

Among the stars, planets
and moons, in the sigh
of our sleepless time,
there you are, they reply.

But I see not me,
no footprint, nor mark
of life's signature
in the spreading dark.

No echo of my voice
returns, and I fear
the words I speak
are but a falling tear.

So it goes, the wind
whispers, so it goes.
The biggest things
Are folded unto a rose.

Carry its beauty
and you carry the world;
and there you live,
your eyes unfurled.

The Rose Within

I didn't know till now
of the distance
in the petals of a rose.

It had always been beguiling,
the beauty and the thorn,
the touch and the nick.

Now the light settles in
its folds as if it has fallen
from the rim of the moon.

It washes against the colours
like the tide against rocks
leaves drops of itself in pools.

It has become the horizon
within that once reached
no longer exists.

It is the silence of a piano
when the keys once played
by the sun are now still.

It is the slant of the sky
deep in the opened bloom
infinity caught for a moment.

Listen

Imagine the voices of the world
now silenced rising
from the earth,
like early morning mist,
wisps of calls, looking
for echoes before
burning off in the sun
and fading out.

Imagine the voice of one
falling, as if no longer
a feather on the wind,
but into the darkness
enfolding
that is the cradle
of stone and soil
and silence.

These passing notes,
this staff of souls,
this ascending
and descending,
this lightness,
this weight
of being human.
Listen.

Two Zeroes

From zero to zero
we span a little thread
vibrate to the sigh
and shout,
the wail and whisper,
kiss and caress.
We are the tremor
in the air that in the
moving is moved.

How can the sum
of it be zero
isn't the question.

The shadow
of our sway
will in time
seep into the
waiting sky,
become the fabric
we once looked
into, and
we
will
be
gone.

How can the sum
of it be zero
isn't the question.
Between two zeroes
was the touch
of the hand
against the clouds,
the trace of a name
in the echo of a
chain of voices,
in the space
between two zeroes.

Call/Response

When the wind rises,
rages and falls
and the dark howl
becomes a stillness
that folds over the day
like a cape.

When the centre
of the turning world
flickers, as a flame,
as a cradling
confirmation
in your open hands.

When your fingers
close around its light
to feel its kindling
warmth, and its shadows
play upon
the air you breathe.

When the pulse of
your heart is the
stream's rhythm
— its burbling wash
and its slow depth
of silence.

Then you will know
the call and response
that comes unbidden
of gazing at the moon,
and feeling only the sun
in the ocean of sky.

River

I am walking on the river bed
for the river no longer flows.
Now it feels the wind and sun
and falling moonlight's glow.

Now under the dry surface it holds
onto the thing it once had been;
the rhythms, pools and stillness,
all to the world unseen.

This is the land of droughts and flooding
rains. This is the landscape passing
within, of ripple and swirl
as one, then vanishing.

Each life is a river.

Nightfall

When the light
fades into the sky.
When the air
settles as a sigh.

When the stars
flick their switch.
When the moon
makes it pitch

to sleep, to sleep:
this is the time
for your dreams
to flow and rhyme

with the rhythm
of a beating heart
with the whisper,
make this start
knowing the wind
will rise,
and the dust will
enter your eyes.

This is the cycle
of nightfall:
before and after,
the sun will call.

The Plaque

Look, this is for you
here is your name
date of birth
date of death
the bookends
of your life
and then a few words
scooped from the sea
washing over us
to be forever
etched into brass
for the sun to kiss
the wind to brush
the rain to touch
the hand to stroke
the smile to bless
the sigh to cause
the heart to rise
and fall.

Look, here is the stone
in the ground
— the mark blood stilled
and blind to the world
that speaks in the silence
with the light of dawn,
with the drawing
of the dark
you were alive

and now are forever
among strangers
among your silent kind
on the edge
of a garden bed
ashes fed, tears watered
where birds peck the earth
where you, undisturbed,
sleep not — for that
is for the living —
but behind our eyes.

Look, here I sit
0n a park bench
an arm's length
from you.
Eternity nuzzles
next to me,
a ribbon of sky
come to earth.
I turn to it,
saying, who knew
you could hold
three years
and today
at the same time.
The ribbon rustles
in the breeze.
But we know,
the graves and
plaques whisper.
We know.

January 2023
The language of grief

There is a horizon in everyone's lives. We carry its distance from the moment of our birth, and on reaching it can no longer describe it. This is journey's end. The final goodbye.

Those left behind are left to describe the landscape of grief and of the life and the death that led to that point. For many it is unfamiliar, and uncomfortable. Some fall to silence, some to distraction, some to creation. Some try to make sense of death's grasp, others merely to seek solace. Of all creatures we mortals are the only ones who can raise our emotions into an articulation of pain and love.

We are, despite everything, social animals, and what binds us are words. Language is the bridge for one soul to cross to another.

In the darkness of grief, how to reach into your heart and mind and extract the words, the right words, to define yourself in lamentation? How to do it with precision, and will your words be received in the same form as they left you?

You have no control over it. You just hope you can sculpt a recognisable shape. But writing and speaking of loss is not a test. It is elemental to being human and some tap into a well, others reside in silence. This, too, is elemental to being human. Sometimes, "No words" speaks volumes.

After the death of my son three years ago, some friends greeted me with those words, and an embrace. It was enough. I knew what they were trying to say; that grief is inexpressible, that coming up against the horizon of nothingness is beyond words.

And yet for three years words have washed up onto the shore. Recently, a mother who had lost her son emailed me to ask if she could use some of my words as part of a memorial to her son. Of course I replied. A little while later she emailed back a photograph of the memorial. This is the resonance of what it means to be human. We are, despite everything, not alone.

There has been no plan, no dotted main points to the words; just a tidal surge of giving voice to thoughts in prose and poems. This is the latest, written as the tide flowed into 2023:

The Weight

Who knew that ashes would weigh the same
in your arms as when you held him as a baby.

You hold them close to your chest,
your heart breaking, this is not something

you were expecting, to be sent back 20 years
to the cradling of love, small soft body

against yours now an emptiness of sky
heavy on your breast.

Each breath is a word, spoken or unsaid,
but what can you say as you place him

in a snug shovel-dug hole in the earth
but keep warm, my beautiful boy.

We brush the plaque now sitting over him
with our fingers — a kiss goodbye of love.

We take a small jar of him home with us.

We have his smile, we say in tear-mist breath.
That night a light rain falls and I think of him

alone in the damp earth. You are not alone I say.

You are not alone.

Grief entered the language, and thus people's lives and deaths, in the early 13th century, the word bereave, meaning to rob, from about 900. Dictionaries point to grief meaning "hardship, suffering, pain, bodily affliction", deriving from the Latin "gravare", meaning make heavy.

Sculpting grief into sentences is both blessing and hardship, for it is a construction of remembrance and love that is built on tears.

The poet Rainer-Maria Rilke saw death and grief as more blessing. In a letter to Adelheid von der Marwitz in 1919, he wrote: "Death, especially the most completely felt and experienced death, has never remained an obstacle to life for a surviving individual, because its innermost essence is not contrary to us (as one may occasionally surmise), but it is more knowing about life than we are in our most vital moments.

"I always think that such a great weight with its tremendous pressure somehow has the task of forcing us into a deeper, more intimate layer of life so that we may grow out of it all the more vibrant and fertile."

Rilke, of course, never met Kerry Packer, who in recounting when he had been clinically dead for a few seconds, said: "I've been on the other side and let me tell you son, there's fucking nothing there."

Perhaps the final words should go to Shakespeare who, in a wildly different context to our ordinary lives, in Macbeth has Malcolm say to Macduff after the latter learns his family has been slaughtered:

"Give sorrow words; the grief that does not speak knits up the o'er wrought heart and bids it break."

AFTERWORD

*It takes a storm to see
the rock beneath the sand,
to feel no more the grains
run through your hand.*

*It takes an ocean to hold
what has been washed away.
Let the waves carry love,
for love is the heartbeat's sway.*

Printed in Australia
Ingram Content Group Australia Pty Ltd
AUHW011808191223
388157AU00003B/3